C0-AVA-168

FEALTY

Ricky Ray

RICKY RAY

First Edition 2019 ©Ricky Ray

All rights reserved.

ISBN: 978-1-939728-31-9

Diode Editions

Doha, Qatar

Richmond, VA

Design & layout: Law Alsobrook

Author photo: Jia Oak Baker

Cover artwork: Shaunna Russell

Ordering & Contact information: http://www.diodeeditions.com

I

II

The earth says have a place,
be what that place requires.

— William Stafford

for
Safora Ray
Ashley Wood
Stanley Nightingale
&
Wendell Berry

.

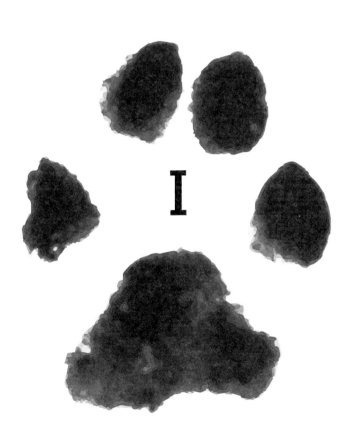

I

What These Senses Can Do

I started in the middle of time,
grew backwards to the beginning
and forwards to the end.

Sometimes the sides switch around
and I feel like I've already stood
where I'm stepping.

Maybe I have, and that's why
the cattails seem so familiar,
windswept over the ancient sand.

Or maybe I'm confused, timeblind,
forgetful, and Mnemosyne's
playing tricks on me.

Maybe that's nonsense.
Maybe the old dog's a fallacy
and the trick is to keep learning

and I, for one,
am still learning
what these senses can do.

The Seven Hundred Sights in a Horse

A wild horse ran through town.
It was always running.
Gospel was: something had
to be wrong with you to see it.
Everyone had seen it.
Those who said they hadn't
kept looking over their shoulders.
Some saw only an eye,
usually when they were blind
to the bad side of a relationship.
Some saw its mane, a mangy sight,
while they took the bus
home from chemo.
Its tongue meant you should
spit the liquor back into the bottle.
The local bum saw its skeleton
as he burned from the hollows
of his eyes. He took up
the guitar again
and strummed until
it disappeared.
Its tail told secrets.
Those who heard the swish
knew what it meant
but could never put it into words.
They said it was like a higher
form of balance. A little girl
put out half an apple every evening.
The neighbor's dog ate it
and she took it as a sign
that she and the horse were friends.
Her mother died young
and she's the only one
who ever saw the horse's heart.

(Or the only one who confessed.)
She married the man
she suspected had seen it too.
He kissed her when she asked.
She and the guitarist became
the resident horse interpreters.
They often disagreed: on its name,
its sex, what color it was,
why it had come to town,
whether it whinnied
when the church bells rang,
what a person ought
to do with what they saw.
Two things they always agreed on:
you only rode it out of town,
and by out of town
they meant out of life,
and if you saw its hoof
you better duck.

When to Reveal

In front of the vet she's stoic
like her papa:
nothing wrong, just give me a treat please,
I mean another one, I mean yeah,
these treats and I have something to settle,
go ahead, you're billing us anyways,
tip over the whole jar.
Don't need to be weighed, my temperature taken,
sure as hell don't need my blood drawn,
imaging,
or to go into the back room. I could pick this building
out of two hundred by a quick sniff at the stoop,
it's not so bad, the elevator smells
and there's urine everywhere,
but those are the joys
a long-nose
lives by. At home, though, I tell my papa:
it hurts, I don't feel so well, help me
on the bed please, it's midnight
but I can't hold it,
this aging thing's a hell of a way to spend
a dog's accumulated wisdom,
or maybe it's some trickster's prep course
all creatures flunk
on the way
to meeting their mama's maker.
Everything won't be alright, let's not lie,
it never was, but another treat
and more where that came from,
a roll in the grass
and a nap in the sun,
and if I don't get up to eat
the giant cookie of the moon,
at least I'll be

the breeze I loved to drink,
and my breath will drift to the edge
of the world, where I'll keep on:
sniffing the stars, digging black holes,
lifting my leg and pissing on the gods' old feet.

Something We Were Supposed to Do

White is the wound of history
crying itself to sleep. Denying it
in the morning. That gives violence
too long on stage. We look at one another
and see the ashes billowing up and out
from under the eyelids. A boy turns to fire.
A girl breaks and no one wants to touch her,
and when someone does, she doesn't
want to cut them, and when she
does, they bleed. The trees twist
in a wind that won't let them grow straight
and our lives look less and less edible.
Even the bears sniff the air
and run away. We live longer
and call it progress. Who knew
the umbilical stink could be strung this far?
And as the species disappear in droves,
we nod our heads and tell ourselves
there was something we were supposed to do.

Note with the Hand I Sent You

for Ashley Wood

Suppose I could spare one.
Hope the left will do
as I'd have a hard time
writing without the right.
To fill you in on its background,
it's always been somewhat wiry,
but don't let that belie its strength;
you can count on it
if you're ever about to fall.
It likes oatmeal and seaweed soaps,
scratching chins,
the occasional massage
in the middle of the palm.
It doesn't like being balled up into a fist
or pointing out faults.
Leave the nails a little long
and, every once in a while,
gaze in wonder at the scars.
On grey rainy mornings,
play it some *irie* music.
When it starts feeling the groove,
give it a dime and the time to tap along.
Offer it a glove as soon as the air
smarts against the cheek.
Keep it happy
with plenty of boob to feel
and it'll gladly help you
carry groceries
when the rest of your hands are full.
And when the world seems
too much, when you
need a hand on your shoulder,
it'll be there—
you won't even have to ask.

Listening

A man, tired after a day's journey, comes to a cabin in the woods and opens the door.

The hinges squeak.
Wings shuffle overhead.

He walks in, waits for his eyes to grow into the darkness, to make out its forms. He finds a stool by a table and sits to rest, not wanting to try his back on the floor. He has no sleeping bag and doesn't feel like piling leaves.

He puts his head
to the table and listens.

It speaks through his skin, his skull, his mind, tells him all he can remember of tables—of wood, trees, seeds and growth, of splinters, termites, rotting and soil. Eventually his mind takes him to the edge of the field where he grows quiet and humble, where his inner voice no longer speaks for the table, and feeling takes over.

He sits there a long time,
until his forehead begins to hurt.

Then he lifts his arm and runs his hand along the edge of the table, slowing to finger its nicks, its rough spots, stopping at the rounded corner. There, in the oily smoothness that might be the inner elbow of someone he once caressed in the night, he grasps the part of the table, the part of the tree,

the part of himself that, then as now,
he does not and cannot know.

In that shadow of time, he belongs to the cabin and falls asleep, waking when his neck grows hot under the morning sun.

If he dreamt,
he doesn't remember.

He listens, not to the table this time, but to the living day—the things he can hear, and the things he can't. The hinges squeak. His stomach grumbles. A box of crackers, quiet as a skeleton, stales in a hidden alcove behind the cupboard.

A small-breasted birdsong
slips under the door.

They Used to Be Things

In the book were pages
and on the pages was ink
and in the ink were words

that were once ideas
we made of things, like
wool is made of a goat

and a *sweater* is made
of wool, and *warmth*
is made of wool's

trappings, and *favorite*
is made of our time
in the warmth.

The story goes
that the ideas
went away and formed

their own tribe. Then,
they forgot to come back
and visit; they forgot

the way home. Over time,
they even forgot
where they came from,

and the more distant
the words grew
from their origins,

the more the words
tried to become things
themselves. But words

are not even the pale
shimmerings on
the butterfly's wings,

let alone the thin
translucence
flapping itself up.

When the wolfwind howls
and the ground
whispers crystals of ice,

if I wrap my feet
in ideas—whole philosophies—
they still freeze.

Even newspaper tucked
into old brown boots
leaves them stiff

and shivering
through the night.
But then I stomp

and chant my confessions
to the moon,
and the rendezvous

of word and blood
lights ten little
fires in my toes.

The Exchange

He sold vegetables from homemade wooden crates,
used sun, soil, seed, water, and a healthy dose of ornery.

I gave him money and my face to remember.
So did my wife. Our dog just gave her face.

We wanted to share his shoes, asked for his wisdom,
which he gave with a crinkle and a joke about moo juice,

said *there's only one piece of advice*
I can give you: grow things.

And now I know there's more to what he spoke,
like: *they'll return the favor.*

Or make it two pieces, he said, *when you find your land,*
learn it like someone you both have married;

find someone who has lived nearby a long time,
and make friends.

On the land, the people grow fewer and few.
Old residents are hard to find.

Neighbors don't make friends if they don't intend
to stick around, or even if they do.

The trust wears thin; the wedding band wears lighter
on the finger; the memory of what happened here,

and where here is, and how here lives,
dwindles in the downturned lamps of people

who take to sleeping in the daytime,
and it stings—that awful, eerie quiet.

So we start again; we root ourselves,
and wait for kin to come.

The Music of As Is

Dearheart: forgive the extreme tardiness of my reply—
I meant to respond much sooner, but, alas, intentions
are weaklings who hardly ever muscle their being
into keeping its appointments. Interesting, the notion
that we're nearly always late to or altogether
miss the meetings set up for us by our desires,
and thereby run around on the stringy detritus
of what could have been. Why stringy? I don't know,
but when I think out the field and walk through its grass,
I envision the shed potential not as flakes of skin
drifting down, but as strung-out guts falling in ropes,
without the gore or macabre mess—no,
these are the guts of something finer within us,
some heavenly-feathered cross-fiber, some
suddening strings of energy that break into music.

When I lie down in that field and feel the wind
make followers of my hairs, I envision us running
over these barely perceptible minnows of failure—visible,
like much of beauty, only if we actively look for them—
and think yes, there's music in the air, so much music
that the strings beneath us and the strings of us
combine and conduct for the ear that cocks
with ache to hear it, and that's the music I want:
the music of the way things go, not the way things
could go, if. Oh, I meant to write you a letter dearheart,
but I guess this is as it should be; I was never much
of a correspondent. Still, imagine the possibilities
of all that music, waiting like starlight to be
plucked, threaded through the ears and taken down.

Old Amber Eyes

The lone owl tucks in for the morning.
He makes the smarmiest sunrise
think it's in a reforestation drama.
He knows his lineage will cease
with the closure of his amber eyes,
but that ruffled feather
has long been shaken down
and settled into a crooked claw.
Why it bends that way.
Extinction in the rot.

A real, live woman is rumored
to have been seen once by the waterfall.
The toucans say the scream
that flew from her bone-white chest
wasn't anything like the legends told.
She fell in when she fell silent
(or did the fall silence her?)
and when we sent the dolphins
to look for what was left of her,
they couldn't find any sign
that she'd ever been.

Arc of an Afternoon

In a stretch of amber water some call the swamps of Florida, a man longs for the home he
has always lived in, a long-muscled wave tossing between shores, the quarter mile of liquid
he knows as if he were the watchman of its vein.

His skin has screamed
the red of so many sunsets

           it sags
           like heavy,
           crinkled leather.

Runs his hand along his scales and nods,
a fish left out too long, lives in longing,

                deepens with a desire
                to forget desire,

takes his lack of satisfaction as a sign
that his work is not complete. He hopes it never is,

that the work which builds in his sleep
            and in his wake

will always rise above him
and shush his noise like water

                —feel turbulent
       in sudden storms—

but day to day surround him
with a constellation
           of swishes
          and suction
that remind him:

man and animal,
manimal and life itself
are members of the elements,
not over-guiding hands that conduct them
                             around
                             an imagined crux,

nor a sweeping swirl of importance
towards which worldly affairs conspire.

Fishing,
            he lifts the reel and twitches
            the line with his finger,
                    feels for the countertug
            that could signify
            a nibble,   a fight,
            dinner and the pursuit of a well-earned swallow:
                    how long the first bite lasts.

In all the sun has wrought of being,
he considers himself a hole,
                        a flute,
                        a stitch along a seam continually resewn,
                        a burst of music,
                        a catch and release,
                        a man who cares what his strokes destroy,
                        a light-footed stepper,
                        a song in a bottle,
                        a living, breathing pore.

Hanging over the edge of his skiff, the salt in his sweat he returns to the ocean. The seaweed
he strips from his line for keeps. The day's work he hammers from memory to muscle to
bone.

The fish he tosses in a gleaming arc

        that says
        goodbye
        and farewell
        and the unsayable
        anguish of entanglement—

the fish he tosses in a gleaming arc

        to another
        half-fated
        chance in the waters.

Dreaming of Panthers

Deep in the Everglades
where a man sleeps with a fan
pointed at his head,
night swallows whatever
the horizon throws at her—
she has no stomach,
it goes right through—
until the sun spreads
its pink invasion
from the corners of the sky
and night's gone—she'll be back.

At dawn a panther
slinks through the sawgrass—pink muhly—
(the day already so
heavy it sinks),
in search of prey, early or late,
perhaps a nine-banded armadillo
coming off the night shift,
the panther's fur rippling,
windteased grain,
muscles undulating down
her tightly-tuned body,
her single instrument—
what but a god could play this?

Does the panther
catch whiff of the stink
of the man? Does hunger push
her face into the crevices
of his shack? Does she crouch
under a thatch of saw palmetto
waiting for the door to open
so she can gauge

his size, defenses,
how he stumbles
out to piss and yawn
at the banana spider
strung between two fronds?

A fog rolls in
with the taste of wild boar
in its heart, which seems
to be the most of it,
banging
from the dream
to tell me a panther
and hunger and a man
drinking himself to death
are forms of a creature
I too inhabit.

I could be any of them.
I could be all.
My body kicks
the covers,
a low growl
rumbles in the throat—
is it phlegm or cat or love?—
a scream tears me awake
and there's blood in my mouth
and I don't know
what happened.

Proximity

The rabbit parts, taken out of the context of the rabbit,
will sit on the counter in their juices, hinting at stew,
and they will look good and hale and nutritious to him,
and they will look like awful, bloody murder to her.

And the differences will hang between them,
not as something to be fought over,
but as something there and real and true.

Something that binds if it doesn't break them apart,
for they will not resolve their differences;
the resolution will come in the way
their differences cuddle one another in the night.

A Neighborhood of Vertebrae

I like to think it would be as easy as saying *I've had enough: pain, leave my body,* and it would pick up and go. It would gather its belongings and take care to leave nothing, not even a breath drawn tightly through the teeth, behind.

It's almost beyond imagining, but to bridge memory to the present, ask. What would it be like to feel comfort again, to wake up and feel pleasure standing, to enjoy the stretch as the hands bring water and wash the face of sleep?

Resist the temptation to answer the question with another question or a solution that dulls the inquiry. There is reward around here somewhere if the tension is followed past the point of a logical conclusion, followed to the source of the problem, even if the problem is a widespread something not right, unclear, probably genetics, or environment, the untold difficulty of living in this body in this world, a dysfunction that fails to fit the paradigms of diagnosis, but quiets down when given a pill whose effect overlaps hurt's song: so much garbled, muscular, nerve-taut rage.

A refrain on repeat, a theme with such potential for variation there is no hope of exhaustion.

A language for one. A book inside of someone who never learned the dialect, who never knew there was such a thing until it started speaking, and if hearing foreign voices in the head, where voices belong, is an indication of a break from reality, what would you think of me if I admitted to hearing the spine speak in ten different tongues?

One for each herniated disc, overlapping grammar
but each with its own syntax
for sending the brain its shades of pain.

Tolerance

We preach tolerance
but beware
the hardenings of exposure:

enough opium to kill a man
would barely
put me to sleep—

impossible to remove
the scars, restore
the veins,

steel wire
that barbs the history
of my hand:

I killed for money
and mercy,
died more than a little each time

but show me the choking weeds
and I will yank them
from their sockets,

show me
the cat's work
in the half-gutted shrew

and I will bring the shovel
down to crush
the egg of its skull again.

On Compassion

After we split the apple with my pocketknife
and ate our way towards the core,
saved the seeds and stem for compost,

she saw a grey lump on the sidewalk,
moved closer and elbowed my ribs,
said *look, is it dead*, and then we

were on top of it, inspecting, looking
for life, movement, any sign that it hadn't
flown the body, but with every part—

the closed eyes, the curled claws,
the wing oddly unfolded underneath—
the answers came back: no, no,

already gone, too late to take death
by the ear and lead it away.
What now I thought,

and *what now,* apparently, she didn't
think, she knew: life brought it to her
and it was hers, one of her own,

said *we have to help it* and that stunned me,
shut me up, made me wonder how
you help something dead,

so I waited for her to show me: she took a napkin
from her pocket, there because she often
has to pee, and picked up the body,

held it close, as though it could still feel her,
said *we need to find a place to bury it*,
and I melted, felt blown apart

by such strength of heart,
so I joined her, scanned the streets
for a paper bag—

paper, not plastic, because it too
would go down in worms—
then I held it open

as she lowered the pigeon
into the breadcrumbs,
a meal for the next life,

or the continuation of this one,
and we forgot our plans
or swept them aside,

made for the park where
a rock became a shovel,
a hole became a grave,

and a man and a woman
buried a fellow creature,
placing flowers on the body

and the roughly mounded soil,
bowing their heads, not in prayer
but in homage of this life

where he fell in love
with the opportunity
to live beside her,

and she in the natural
course of her compassion
learned that he

would hold up
his end of the work
when it came time to do it.

Way of the Bear

Have the ghosts lost touch or have we lost the art to hear them?

The way of the bear stays in the bear, though we wear its head
and coat as we chant and pray to the forces for guidance. Maybe,
if we sit with thought until it breaks quietly over the blaze
of attention, if we sit with hunger until the names for things recede
into their whispered collaboration, the eyes will glaze and clear

and shift from one sight of truth into another: we'll look down
and see the fur, dark and shaggy along our arms, the claws sharp
and lethal at the tips of our fingers, the green asleep in our bones
till spring, the light awake in our bones till sleep, the dead
as murmurers of mystery in the language of the living;

and we'll stand so still in the water's rush that fish and stones
and force of hunger converge as figments of the river's song,
and the way that stays most days within the bear will awaken
in the one-part human, standing in the one-part earth;
and we'll sway like a wave cresting in the autumn breeze,

crashing in upon itself, a wave that enters the mouth of a fish
caught between two swift paws, lifted into the morning light,
switching rivers from water to flesh, yes—we'll stand in that
lost art of living where the bear tears open the body of Chinook
and we of the imagination catch ourselves breathing its breath.

Two Postcards to Myself from April 1, 2017

I

Good morning, Sunshine. Not that one opens a lost missive in the morning, and is the good a wish, a curse, or an observation? A cold-fingered hand around a warm mug of coffee, a burnt-sugar soul ground out of Ethiopia. Enough of a pilfer to face the day. Hell of a cold rain last night. Hours without an umbrella, another quarter in the downpour before an empty cab. The chill went to bed with you, slept in the cush of your marrow. Now your skin is dry, but your bones, still wet with it, still wet with the ocean they crawled out of, clamor for fire. Give them the splinters of your mind. And a match.

II

Let them rise and come out of your poem, failed, the one that said the clouds hung heavy and low, a blue to them you couldn't name, something between periwinkle and sky. This is taking two postcards because you're longwinded. The horses are up and quartering the little muscles in your back. The cats are sleeping with the dog and the dog is running on better knees in her sleep. All those years in the city. Think of the trees you could have had outside your window, the forms of thirst revealed after lifetimes of drinking light. Is thirst ever quenched, or merely shed like old skin? Maybe having one's fill is beside the point, and one of the virtues of experience is that it belongs to an art of waking up.

When You Lost It

Tell me the day drowned in you,
his half-dead desire ripening
fuchsia and violet into the river
where you watched your life
sunset over the Jersey shore.
Or one of your lives. One of the people
in your person put to bed. You were
young when you first saw this,
old enough to have attempted
suicide, to touch the failure
as one in a long line of scars—
the little slugs on the wrist,
the kisses on the knees,
the thinning in the left eyebrow
where the curb almost took you
into the pavement—each scar whiter
than the skin it occupied, the brushes
of death leaving ghosts to remind us:
defeated warriors are always
walking home. Two-puff cigarette butts
appearing here and there
like winter flowers on their journey.

*

Tell me the day drowned in you.
Tell me you threw yourself
like a fish into the sea and covered
yourself in all the oil we ever spilled
and all the oil we ever took.
Tell me you swam into the mouth
of a whale who took you to see
his wise old soul before he spit you out
clean within sight of the sharks,

transformed. Tell me you listened
to the homing device in your chest
as you sprouted arms and legs.
Tell me you swam for your life,
scrambled up naked on the beach
and fell back on the sands,
so happy, so fucking happy
to call breath your greatest currency.
Tell me you swore you'd spend your days
teaching children how to swim.

Forbidden Diamonds

We didn't play for keeps. Money never changed hands.
No one packed lunch: the diving catch with the bases
loaded and Joey coming up with a bruised rib—

that we ate all day. For spectators, we had our silent,
spitting hearts. The shadow women waiting at home
in our socks. We wanted every pitch to smoke,

every swing to smack the whole world over the wall.
After a while the score didn't matter. The toe in the dirt,
Raul's wild arm, the pigeon that shat on first base:

it was always and only the play. I batted for both sides.
Couldn't catch for dick. Stepped up to the plate
and everyone shut it. It was something

to something, we were squinting in the dusk,
and we all shouted at the guard to wait a fucking
minute as he threatened to call the cops. I imagined

Johnny was throwing me the guard's fat head, a slider,
teeth first, slick with the grease of his polyester
sweat—they said I swung so hard I broke the air.

Despair

Say *stay alive*. As though
your blood weren't saying it.
As though your senses
weren't listening. As though
you had a choice. Buck against
the closed mouth caging
the wild animal of your tongue.
Call the sun a sadistic source
and rage the whole day through.
Then fall against the teeth,
old and holey but strong enough
to chew you down to size.
Fall not in defeat but exhaustion.
Curl up in the remnants of the curses
you hurled across your lips,
the sounds falling around you
like names, pinched possibilities,
the settlements of sallow cells.
It's a good place to be broke.
You can suck the sour candies
of your sores. You can watch
the clouds pass through your head
and dare them to break hell loose.
You can oven yourself to bake the blues.
You can raise the corner of one lip
or two when the dawn dies
and your veins report
a good night's work distilling light
to replace the gold life looted.
Life's a digger. She has no
scruples. She'll take the teeth
out of your mouth. She'll loan
you breath, belief, the apparition
of will, a disrepair of bones.

She'll collect whenever she wants.
She won't listen to reason.
She'll take it all.
She'll give a little back.
She'll pry your name off
your tongue. She'll soup
your guts. She'll slurp.

Kifka

for Kazim Ali

Kismet, fate, karma: not pre-determined—
there is no before or after to one
who stands or wavers or buzzes
throughout and beyond time—
but self-determining,

the net or web or ocean of infinity,
where our senses and abilities
and the extent of our detection
succumb to their limits
and it all rests

on the tip of your nipple, on the pull
of tides within you, on the tide
you are within this, on the systems
in which notion collapses,
experience collapses,

holes disappear

and the air at your lips is the universe
giving you the opportunity
to kiss it,

giving itself lips and you
to do the kissing,

giving itself
itself
to be kissed,

or not.

The Word Want

for C.C.

First, let's start with what we don't want.
We don't want a dichotomy
that splits us into boys and girls
who don't fit the picture perfect.
Men and women of questionable intent
who sneak around in the middle of the night.
A tangle of limbs, an aversion to deviants,
a counterculture forming the category
of merger that no one wants to talk about.

What we want is a blurring of the lines
where the boundaries overlap,
sharp reliefs where the areas
of overlap solidify our relations.
We want a language of the grey area
where acceptance is a prerequisite
and is thus rendered a meaningless fact.
We want actions that stand for themselves,
actions that don't have to justify why they exist,
but are willing to explain themselves
if someone wants to understand.

We want children that want to be doctors
and educators, or else undercover assassins
that will rid the world of evil;
and if our children can't figure out
whether they want to heal, teach or kill,
we want them to build and maintain societies
or attend to the breaking of rules.
We want failures to succeed as artists and farmers,
losers to ascend into middling management,
and we want the disabled to show us
what we don't know about ourselves,
what hellfire slumbers in that fleeting twinge.

We want people who deeply feel
and just as deeply care,
and we want them to do something smart
with all of those useless feelings.
We want truth and justice and beauty,
and we want death death death
to take a hike hike hike. And then,
we want to know death as the backbone of life,
to grow old with it like a spine
that takes a lifetime to open and flower.

We want to feel firm in the conviction
that everything happens in love,
even the hatred that spits in the face
of everything we've meant so far.
We want to overcome all of our hidden
resentment and malevolence,
be it towards the mirrors on the walls
or the mirrors eating and breathing
everywhere around us.

We want our vulnerability
to be as valuable as immortality,
and the sense to recognize
that it always was.
We want to go forth without pain,
and since pain is unavoidable,
we want to take pain with us
to where it will no longer
be able to hurt.

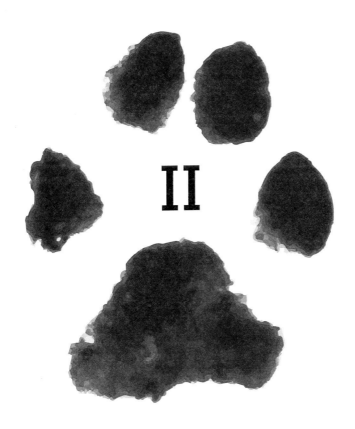

Guard Dog

for Sergio Ortiz

Mother me, rain, I come home
tired and thirsty
down to the snake-hiss of my bones.

No one to water my roots,
I rode them
to the river and told them *drink*.

My life sounded like a dog
trying to quench
the aridity of the west:

only marginally inhabitable,
he had perpetually
dusty eyes.

That dog has died
and I've buried him
too many times to tell.

And every time I climb in his grave
till he rises
to walk me home.

Even now, when I lay quiet as earth
under the clouds,
I can hear in my heart

the lap-lap, lap-lap
of that long, insatiable tongue.
He watches over me:

at the smell of whiskey on my breath,
he lifts his head to bark the liquor
back into the grain.

The Lightbulb

The lightbulb in the hallway had trouble making connections.
I was hopeless to help him, too short to reach the ceiling,

my ladder lent to an ex who never returned it.
There were signs that something was wrong.

His friend the fly visited less and less frequently.
I thought it a lull in the warmth of their companionship.

For days, I'd come home, flick his switch, and he'd wave at me—
not at all his style. He was more the type to shroud.

Then I tried him yesterday morning and he wouldn't move.
Three shakes later, he opened his eyes. Obviously,

the end was near. I felt depressed. I'd taken a shine.
I liked the way he made the letters stand out against the page,

the shadows he cast as Safora lowered her breasts into the bathtub,
how he blended with the day but, come nightfall, could rival any star.

On the train home last night, I imagined grieving processes
for bygone sources of light. I opened the door.

My finger trembled as I groped along the wall.
An inch later his sole synapse misfired and everything went dark.

Through the Veil

A woman sings, *when I was born,*
I stepped through the veil. Her mother
and father are myths she's still making.

His dark skin, whether sun or melanin,
darkens as his Harley thunders
down the highway, sweat in his beard,

a single point in his mind where
she could curl up and fall asleep.
Her mother has scars on her back

from where they removed the wings.
No angel, she studied the butterflies
and joined them; was caught the day

she picked up her legs and flew.
The woman's friends trust her with secrets.
She puts them where she came from:

she cannot reveal what she never knew.
When she waves goodbye with the light
behind her, her friends mistake her hands

for birds. They are, but she holds them in.
She's afraid of giving birth. As a child,
she couldn't find herself in the color wheel,

so she turned to soil, and in the sundown silt
where her legs became flippers in the delta,
she found her hue. She asked it, *why?*

It said something she couldn't hear.
In her dreams, the words are coming
clear as the coal cries in the mountain,

mixing men with rock as the tunnel
folds, the pressures of life
forcing us to bear diamonds.

They will be taken in blood.
She tells the birds in her to build
their nests over the shiny parts.

The Bloody Medium

Bless the man who carries
the child down the stairs,
a piranha chewing
his lower back.
The mother hauling
diaper bag, stroller,
cheap Orchard St. suitcase,
the sudden absence
of a husband, eviction
notice stickered to the door.
The lights went off
three nights before.
The bright, cold day
felt new. Its magnetism
lit her feet. She thanked
the man, declined
his offer of further escort.
The subway, yes, she had fare.
She didn't, but knew
the guard and liked her
chances. The boy was cute
and quiet. She wore no
make-up, didn't need it
with those eyes.
The boy asked where
they were going.
She said she had asked
God that morning,
was still listening
in her blood
for the answer.
He wondered how
God got in her blood.

Paradise

Why I left paradise? The people were none too friendly. This should come as no surprise. I mean just because you put people in idyllic situations doesn't mean they behave ideally. They still have stomachs and brains, private parts and the tendency to poorly use them. They still stink. They still strive to be better than they are, and fail, and strive again. They still give up. They still succeed. I'm right alongside them, a face in the crowd that only a handful could ever pick out. I see children dashing toward the playground, the wind in their hair, the joy on their faces turning sour when the ball doesn't spin their way, something all too spoilt taking the place of joy as a boy yanks ponytails left and right. He needs a good kick in the balls.

I see men and women with humility in their veins and happiness in their hearts watching children play, and I see men, mostly men, watching young girls and wishing they could play with them. I see people with hearts in their heads feeding pigeons, and people with hearts shriveled up telling them they are wrong to feed. The admonishers have nothing better to do. Life, for them, is an avenue that smells like piss and an alleyway full of bums who shouldn't exist. Good whiskey and a bad heart. Good intentions and a bad lot. Why should they let the world be at peace? Why shouldn't they expect bouquets in return? Something tells me if they had the guts to get down and peck amongst the pigeons, they would, and they wouldn't be nice about it, either.

Some days, I would join them. Some days, I would run at them with my arms spread like a hawk to scare them off. Nice, not nice, it's a matter of moods. It's an alternating current. The blood boils, the blood cools. Sleep prevails, passion falters. The life-weight etches. The life-force erases. We attempt to matter. The matter we are thwarts us. We get it and forget it. The eyes open and close. They look out and look in. We know what we think and don't know what to make of it. We hurt and want anything else. Here, my life, one day, I'll trade you. I'll probably regret it. So will you. I'll hope it isn't true but prepare to accept the hopelessness of the situation.

How does one make such preparations? We're ready for whatever happens. We have no hand in it but the hands we have. I'm trying to feel something and put down the feeling so someone can come along and pick it up. I leave off at the fingertips. I must. I must because

I choose, because the choice is made. Act is passage. It goes both ways. Intention is given to take up. I look at you and see myself. You look at me and see yourself. The heart races. Vibration rises. The air becomes palpable between us. We both sense it and then we are, we're touching. We always were. We need only remember how.

Bloomin'

Neighbor, someone ought
to take those fireworks and shove
them up your flower.

A Thousand Palms a Day

At the ticket window,
an elderly woman,
her face so tired it falls asleep without her,
takes your palm instead of your money,
cuts it open with a knife that doesn't hurt,
and reads the code in your blood,
really a story within a story,
a furred creature running across the page
with letters for footprints, and *hurry up*, you think,
stick to his heels, the rain's coming,
he's already a dark spot on the horizon,
you'll miss the point of yourself
if you don't read what he said in his tread!

But she still has your hand
and when you try to pull it away
you fondle her inner organs
and she moans something in a language you can't repeat,
each moment erasing itself, you can't repeat,
and when you quit fidgeting so she can do her thankless job,
your hand comes out without any fingers attached.
She picks up each digit, peels it like a piece of fruit,
then rewraps it as carefully as a newborn
and hands it back.
You plug them in like thumb drives,
scars and arthritis and the muscle memory
of how to throw a dart intact.

She stops at the last pinky, her eyes move aside,
and a strip of 8mm film runs through the sockets,
showing you snapshots of yourself in the womb…
The hours flicker, and the sun seems to be
waiting for her signal to close the day,
waiting until you understand
each of the shapes in your fingerprints,
and when you do, you can tell she's a mother,
the mother in fact of everyone you ever knew,
smiling the smile of 1,000 palms a day for sixty years
with no days off, and it makes you want to wee yourself,
and she nods and says *go ahead dearie, look down,*
what else did you think the drain was for?
But just your wee, mind, don't try to go with it.
Life isn't done with you yet.

Because Meaning Physics Life

Being aware of awareness has become,
like liquor or liking too much, hard to handle,
and when we walk through skins
or kinds of consciousness,
dark fills in our footprints
with the insistence of matter:
a little dirt picked up,
a little skin left behind,
the impression of having been.

Something wants to call it wayward,
then doubts what it wants.

The tongue's a question-mark
that answers itself in the mouth
because the causeless cures reason,
and dried-apple pies taste
sweetest after too many hours
flattening one's metatarsals.
A bark becomes a kind of hello
one throws like stones:
to see what comes back.

Because love runs us over,
we imagine the uses of roadkill,
a little flatter each *thunk*,
a talisman to carry
in one's pocket
until someone arrives
who carries its other side.

Walks are sketches. The scratch of heel
along a path ten-thousand worn.
No way to paint this. A day and another
and they fail to acknowledge
a difference. If there was one, it stopped
for a drink and stumbled bleary
into blue-eyed dawn,
the slosh of heartbreak in its shoes
healing each hurt step.

The Enmity Between Spiders and Bees

after Carol Ciavonne

This is what it meant to [*xxxxx*]*.

The spiders crawled up her tresses—
this is before they were spiders,
before they had six-shooters—
and she said *take my hair into your legs,*
spin it a ghostly gossamer and swing.
They bit her dead, ate the evidence;
they couldn't risk her revealing their secrets.
She sat still and let them. She struggled
and let them. Her body shat
and let them burrow into her eyes.
The cellular screams that ripped her
swift as hummingbirds on the scent of sugar
were precisely what she wanted
when the hive of her belly
glowed red as a coal
and burst with the unappeasable anger of bees.

*Clap five times
 for the words that have died
 and left strangenesses in the tongue.

Calls Them Kin

Easing up her nights of terror,
secrets sweated and sucked back,
she wakes with hands
that make minor pancakes
of the light. Feet that spawn
deliveries the color
of yes you. And you and you
and no, not you: don't ask,
you damn well know.
Let it all be felled away,
the feathers fall from flight.
And yet away, elsewhere's if,
still beads her blood,
where feathers fluff;
she bids them bleat,
they half obey,
she half-obeisant lets them be;
and flight that flew
from bird and good
curls up in her for lack of fur;
she tucks them in,
calls them kin:
the errors of her life.

One Day Becomes Forever

How good to take root, for once,
in the grit of spoiling grace.
To get down and sniff
in search of the scent of prey.
And find nothing,
tramp home heavy
with the hunt's failure,
pass the empty sack
from hand to hook in rumpled quiet,
the hook that sags from the sack alone,
the wood holding 3 out of 7
edges of the screw,
the crack in the wood lengthening
like lightning come to claim,
the window creaking in the wind
with the sediment of yesterday
and the thousands before it,
each an emissary of understanding—
no woman but the half within,
no fresh kill but the cells
that deliver themselves
to the need for a broom—the water,
almost too much to drink,
pours a lullaby half-river, half-rain,
and the pot of beans
heated for the fourth day
on the stove:
how could such seduction
answer the question of the nose?

Animalis

for Rosmarie Waldrop

I woke up this morning feeling fur, asked myself
what I was dreaming. A certain silkiness to the touch
denied dog, felt feline even if the skin underneath
was human. My tongue went to my teeth but they

felt like my old nubs. I took a breath and my nostrils
whistled their proper deviations. Arched my back,
and *that* felt too good for a spine so ruptured and wrong,
so I put off the mirror, put off the inevitable collapse

into person, walked back towards the darkness, told
the mind to be quiet—*shhh*, we're asking Egyptian spirits
what it takes to awaken claws in the fingers, to restore
the tail as rightful rudder, to call us back to the animal

we never left. The answer I got was a hiss and a purr,
a hum in the belly that played along the body like
a reconfiguration of the ribs. A reminder: to stay low,
remember all fours, feet that know the earth and never

wonder how to walk it; to sniff first and listen hard,
haunches coiled with instinct when prey can be
felt ahead in the bushes; to swallow with neither
guilt nor glee, just one life consumed, and then,

if luck stays with us, another; to chew grass
when something spoils and the stomach needs
to be purged; to chew cornhusk for no reason other
than it's good and bears repeating, and remembering

in the limbs, where many things are remembered:
the trees of old properties; mice holes of apartments;
the kittens who went walking and never returned;
the smell of dumpsters and oceans that could break

this nose open; the feel of sunlight in the desert
where once we were gods, parting the sands as our
footsteps left water, unafraid of our shadows, unafraid
of our powers, unafraid of the earth's insistence

that we live nine times to protect her heart.

Confirmation

Entering the temple of the forgotten oracle, she seems to be caught in the sleep of the lifeless. A leaf drifts from the shadow of a branch to our feet, a note scrawled thereon in hasty cursive:

do not wake me
I have given your language to the lower orders
your species descends its mountain having never reached the top

you have managed your gift poorly
you would put off the end
but the furious invention of self-sabotage is all that remains

you have occasionally shown great courage
despite your talent for neglect and ruin
turn back and attend to the creatures who will survive you

you will know them by their fear

Thanksgiving with Vegetarians

In a field, somewhere out west, where an eagle feather
refuses to land, and hunger is a constant occurrence,
and the thunder of bison can still be felt in the rumble

of the iron horse as it chugs down the line—out west
in a land of wheat and rust, where fear of late blight
hangs like a fog over Scandinavian dreams, dinner

is a brown paper bag, a sandwich and an apple within:
two slices of Wonder slathered in PB&J, grape,
the kind that has never known the shortening of days

on the vine—who knows what it really is, who knows
what wasteful state the mind was in when it conjured
disposable jars—and as they swallow the stale crust,

they remember the ham they refused on principle
in Tompkins Square, then they turn to the main course,
a meal they have prepared in love a thousand times,

knowing each taste could be their last. They huddle
over the spoon and the flame, she cradles the solitary
needle like a line of communication between the flesh

and the divine, joy dances in the firelight reflected
in their eyes, and the poppy milk sings in the veins
of the downtrodden, their bodies slump to the ground,

the ass-cracks of passed-out heroin addicts hold court
with the waxing moon, and their lips turn blue
as the waters of tropics kiss miles of coral goodbye,

and the Braeburn rots in the wrinkled brown bag,
and the grey wolves growl as the winter wind howls
and calls the vultures down to their Thanksgiving feast:

young, chilled, slightly spoiled vegetarian lovers
on the bone—bedded by blood, six feet of genocide,
scalped earth, lively with spirits and worms,

the tattoo of an eagle feather on her ankle, molting,
catching two quick puffs of breath, then landing where
the bridge that life built beckons them into black rain.

The Need for a Sickly Body to Rebel: All It Takes is One Overambitious Limb

for Cormac McCarthy

1. The world is a dangerous place and my kids are the reason I water it down.

    a. I have only known myself to be in mortal danger twice, and neither time was I aware of my impending peril.

        i. Courage is a strong suit in a meeting full of soft, unoffending bodies.

    b. I have no kids.

        i. Whose kids are the kids who have no parents, biological or otherwise, if not yours and mine?

    c. My reasons for abortion include the horrors lived by the little children of my mind.

        i. Who isn't prone to dressing up one's notions in the miseries of the world?

    d. I fear for the souls of my soul and the scar tissue that could hamper the development of their mind-muscle early on.

        i. They can taste it in the water, detect my fear and my deception; they pick up the sugar, look at me as upon a child, sigh and say *you know, it's okay, you can give it to me straight.*

2. The danger I see in the world, I sense in myself, and I'm not sure your life is any safer in my hands than mine is in its occupation of society.

    a. I have inflicted harm more times than I ever want to remember.

        i. I do not know what I will demand of myself when I want nothing but the truth.

    b. Doubt is a dagger in the best-laid plans of trusting companions.

        i. Yes, the wrinkles that aren't ironed out will have to be worn out and we're full of the warmth and the sweat it takes to do it.

    c. Hands that lie still do as much harm as the hands of harm they do not seek to quell.

        i. At the sight of violence, how often does one feel the tremble to violently shove that act right back where it came from?

    d. There was no place carved out for me, and yet I have always found room enough to be little bothered and breathe.

        i. Not everyone is so lucky, and of what good is excess fortune if not to be shared?

3. The common lot is all too easily disowned, and at times poverty hurts so much it seems that even the self is a kind of crime.

    a. Someone said in my head recently that *every man is tabernacled in every other and he in exchange and so on in an endless complexity of being and witness to the uttermost edge of the world.*

        i. The sight of blood spilling incites a judgment every heart beats the simplicity of (no matter how quickly the head refuses to look).

    b. The coupling of providence and necessity gets hacked to pieces by the collection of things.

        i. If the body can do without and withstand, so can its inhabitant, and so can the peculiar hue of the inhabitant's mood.

    c. Identity demands an other, and rightly so, but if that other cannot be welcomed within this sphere, someone will have to go.

        i. All wheres of the human body share the route of bones, flesh and blood; broadening the distance between warring members, though it may bring quiet, will not bring peace to the space between us.

    d. Everyone is deserving, did what it took to be here or, earnings aside, here happens to be.

        i. Losing sight of the commonwealth, the health of the part can lead to the disease of the whole, and if the other parts stand to suffer from it, they will (and should), of course, rebel.

4.   A fourth question rises, half-formed, something about the weakest link, and the power of the links around it to restore, voice by voice, fist by fist, stitch by stitch, its, which is to say our, strength.

      a.   A body that is not well will first attempt to right itself through peaceful measures, but if those measures prove ineffective and its health continues to worsen—if it has to declare war on itself, it will, and the body will not stop until the body itself falls still.

Blue Hurricane

She was blue and it hurt
because she wanted to be white—
not Caucasian, mind you,
but any color she pleased.
Her lovers were multifarious:
cat, cotton, cappuccino,
Mr. Cambridge, and Cornell
from Georgia who called his mama
every Friday like the breeze.
She wanted the Middle and Far Easts
to settle down in her lower abdomen,
but she was blue, and as the jazzman
blew his horn, naked from the waist up
on the corner of Houston and 1st,
her shoulder strap fell,
and she wished the rest
of her dress, wished desire itself
would follow. And the liquor
bottles jangled their song
of emptiness from the gutters.
And the mouse took
the moldy bread home.

Just a Moment

I stop, soul, somewhere, waiting for you
to catch up, and looking back I see
your face buried in the flowers of memory,
your nose deep in the branch inhaling
twenty springs in a snort. How's the high?
Grey winter contaminations? The year
half the sparrows froze and fell? The noise
of them breeding back to their former glory?

Come up, soul, horse, eater of bruises
and apples, I need your ancient nose
to tell me the what of am, your noble
nostrils to remind me that no scent
captures the dog, who, *ruff*, lingers
over the stain, pays her urine, trots on.

Four Contracting Sentences and Two Scenes that Won't Comply

I

That day on the farm with the peach
big as a hambone stripped down
to marrow and flavor,
the little heres-and-theres aunt Gertrude adds
that make all the difference,
that get lost in the process
of moving out and moving on,
go down as the missing ingredients
of a tradition that, if we close our eyes
and allow the drift, we can still taste,
maybe even identify
if we catch memory off its guard.

II

The potentials in our natures
we've yet to activate
saying don't forget we're here
while you're busy with other
lovers whose promises
sound more enticing
than our meager requests for work,
work and hints at an eventual payoff
that, if you're lucky,
you won't be too old and decrepit to enjoy.

III

Always less and more than what came before:
less than the Earth who of herself produced us,
more than the history whose landscape
spreads out beneath our feet,
our travels the newest points
of its ever-expanding universe,
pigeon-toed, pecking at seed, gamey.

IV

Body revolving around body,
keeping their distance and keeping the order,
coming together and upsetting the balance
and we can't have that, now, can we?

V

Across the way on a window ledge,
pigeons interlock beaks
and bob their heads up and down.

Have you ever seen two birds kiss?

He jumps on her back and quickly jumps off.
She casts him a look and flies away.
Something wasn't working,
an octave above and an octave below our hearing,
he alone and I alone,
the music not meant for mortal ears.

VI

Their siblings who live in my wall
won't stop cooing
and I'd break their necks if I could.
It's been that kind of day. Syntax, hungover,
unfriendly, refuses to give an inch
so you want to rub it out
and lounge in the space it leaves behind.

Then, a walk out in the after-rain
and, seeing one drink from a dirty curbside puddle,
I'm so touched in the heart
I raise my hand to check for the shaft of an arrow.

No shaft, no arrow, I can only hope
the heart it didn't pierce wasn't all in my head.

Thank You

A wing in the wheat, no blood.
The tank's nearly empty
and no one's pruning the family tree.
This isn't a good idea. We ought to worm.

I know a field where love was born,
it came out screaming,
hungry as heaven for the eyes of hell,
hell for the mythical liquor tit.

The mess milk's made.
To put a dream in the oven
and listen to it sing.
Stone: the sky that fell so hard.

Quartz: the record of where the angels fought back.
Belief: mending a shattered wing.
In the ledger of why we stuck together,
there was no mention of diamonds.

I taste fate every time I swallow:
seaweed, bourbon, bile.
I spit at taunting death
and hear a star in my head say *thank you.*

I Saw Myself in the Black Car

for C.D. Wright

Teardrops on the armrest, the driver wore white gloves,
and the tires, new, unpebbled, sang in the steam rising
from the road. In the quiet of loss, you could hear the sighs,

the four-part breaths collide in brief accidents of harmony.
You couldn't hear the hurt, though if you were a spirit
flitting from heart to heart, you could warm yourself

in the grief. The driver wore his in his foot, tore after
the horizon as after a secret that would make the difference
between an end that shreds the mind, watches strands

of memory flutter down, and one that slides out whole,
a full life risen in the body's kiln. The difference
between a senseless void and hello my friend old black.

One truth says: goodbye to the red river of blood
is all there is to dying. Another truth calls each end
a homecoming, blood's seep into the earth, where blood

is washed of salt and deed, then blood runs strong and clear
on the long road to the sea, where salt returns. There it churns,
prepares to be lifted, an uncertain forecast, almost rain,

breathfine droplets, goldflaked and glistening, sunspit
that waters the day-young sky, a maker's mist that falls over
the windshield of the black car and sings under its tires again.

The Bird

I

She looked over and saw a bird
underneath a city tree, its head sunk,
its body so still and low we thought it dead.

Then it struggled to lift its head and showed us:

one eye swollen, an inlaid marble,
the other swollen and crusted over,
the beak grotesque with infection.

It wobbled its head and shook
as though a fault line were widening,
and it was.

II

Her heart leapt out of her
and I felt it
and mine followed.

Then I acted out of pain and frustration,
that sobering, sorrowful uselessness,
told her to get up, I wanted action,
said sitting there being sad
was doing nothing to help it,

and that was true, or maybe it wasn't,
but it was the wrong way to say it,
the wrong way to harness this energy
hovering over a life that was broken and breaking apart.

We carried our groceries upstairs,
called the rehab center and left a message.

Got down the cat carrier,
made a nest out of socks and an old t-shirt,
a nest we'd made before, and told the cats to be good.

III
She cupped it,
lowered it into the nest, covered it,

told me how cold it felt,
and bony: even less of a chance.

I found the hand warmers,
shook them and placed them
over its wings.

She filled a Japanese
iron tea cup with water
and dripped drops along its beak.

We couldn't tell if it swallowed,
tried to decide what to do,
turned to the internet for help.

It didn't offer much.

IV
Then I heard commotion
in the cage, saw it flapping
and called her over.

Maybe the warmers were too hot,
or maybe it wanted freedom,
from here, from its body, from life, just—out.

She held it again,
tried to shush its heart calm.
It settled for a moment.

Then it flapped, harder,
flipped itself over, clawed
at some invisible enemy in the air.

We saw the gash along its body,
how wasted its flesh,
felt its inability to eat and she made the call.

V

I had no doubt in the right of her heart.

Something in me knew this was coming,
forefelt the tears in her eyes,
the dread in my limbs.

I found the sharpest, largest knife I could
and hid it along the arm of my sweater.

She asked if I was going to break its neck.
I shook my head, said I wasn't confident
that would be quick and painless;

what I had in mind would be quicker and sure.

VI

She asked if she could carry it to the roof,
and I said yes, picked up a plastic bag for after.

Then she asked if she could help,
and I said no, wanted to spare her that,

and she didn't protest or ask again,
walkèd to the other side of the roof and cried.

VII

I held it down on a flat rock,
its head drooping on that mangled neck,
felt the strength in its muscle
as I pinned it down

—so faint—

pressed the blade gently but steadily into its throat,
its incandescent, purple-green, grey-feathered throat,

and sliced,
quick and hard,
in one swift stroke
severing spine and head
and leading its blood towards the light.

VIII

God, how that headless body writhed,
bucked for minutes against
the stillness that called it out of this world,
or down through its seams
into the underbelly of existence,

and no wonder it shook:
all that energy leaving the body at once.

I walked over and hugged her then,
saw her wet, red, swollen eyes
and felt pangs I have no words for.

IX

I asked her to get napkins,
two more plastic bags.

She did. I cleaned,
kept the head with the body
and wrapped it in white.

She saw the knife
on the way down and knew.

X

Later that day,
she said a good man
is better than a great one.

I know what she means.
And when she says it,
I believe her.

XI

I went up the next morning
to check the spot:
all that was left was an already fading,
poorly wiped-up pool of blood.

That, and something I couldn't name,
something that passes between us in times like these,
something that made my whole body tingle with affection
when I went back down and watched her sleep.

Spring Again

Under the cherry trees we visit
the last week of every April,
come by train and foot to celebrate
the renewal of the years,
under blossoms bombing
bodies that grow more quiet
but no less ebullient in their celebration,
Addie rests her snowy chin across my shin,
sighs and settles her sumptuous snout
into a nap. If I didn't know better,
I'd think a visitor from the sun
had placed his hand there,
and that his warmth was telling me
something I should know.
In turn, I too close my eyes,
return to the earth, and place my hand
on the marvel of her knee,
asking it to wait ten thousand days
before it hurts again. And this,
the transference of fealty,
not words, is the language we use
when we to talk to each other
on either side of sleep.

A Graveyard

A walk that was weary until the clearing came into view. Not the eerie quiet one might expect, but the dead quiet of a birdbath attended by no birds, ants excavating a skull under a windless sky. Flowers, dead too, except for the wild ones—among *them* a mixture of the living and the dying, the hellions and hallelujahs, singing the soil, side by side.

Bouquets and single roses, bunches of hyacinth and phlox, marigolds and coxcomb. Something else unnamed and poisonous. Broken liquor bottles and beer cans. Someone has been here, someone has left these tokens of affection, or derision, someone may be watching—from which side of the divide? If a divide, if.

A graveyard, because there are stones, fallen, heads on a platter, and something underneath— the width of a baby, withered at the breast, the width of a man, his hands done with touch. Stones cut and engraved, topped by arcs that resemble trajectories of lives—over and across, into the waters, like stones that someone, or something, has thrown.

The faces of the stones shorn of details,
except to say: *someone lies here—*
time and weather have
erased the meaning of who.

Someone cared, someone who stood these stones upright to testify to the breaking of hearts over the burying of bodies. Someone who died, away from here, who couldn't watch the stones fall, or right the fallen stones, which testify to the falling of the bodies around those hearts, too.

And here, in the thud of footsteps, as in the tapping of an invisible finger on the skull—a thud heard now, though it hasn't been heard for years—a whisper, that you too will fall, and everyone you know, and all the houses you have lived in, and these woods, this planet, this galaxy, and then, who knows…

Maybe what started it all will see to its end, might even then remain, might stir, might be so restless in its thirst for being, for movement, that it sings from the stone, the dust, the last disappearing speck, and sends it all reverberating again.

III

Bounty

The old hat on the hook
with its moth-eaten holes
letting in more than light.

Someone's Ashes

Maybe it hurts to be someone
and the sky is a lung
viewed from the inside. She smokes
because she can. She's stupid
because she smokes. He digs
in his pocket for love
but all he has is a lighter.
There are better breaths
than truth. Companionship
comes equipped with holes
for lies. Better to be burnt
by those little spurts of steam
than boil down to dark forever.
The days drift like leaves
that no one rakes.
Our lives hitch along
like sleepy embers.
The wick of time
burns hot at our heels:
what do we expect of ash?

A Glass of Kentucky Heresy at the Window

My hip says it's going to rain. The wind blows
from the west with whiskey on its breath.
The floorboards have warped for too long
and *Oma's* heart's about gone, but I don't complain.

I still have my mane and most of my teeth,
and most of my children are still on their feet.
The ones who pick up a pen and write, anyways.
Been too long since we heard from Johnny or Julie,

and I never liked that husband of hers. Always
seemed like a bum with those two idle thumbs
and reluctance to work. Never did thank us
for that shirt. Guess he's too good for manners,

but listen to me, passing judgment under the Lord.
Let he who first, and Lord knows I ain't without sin
or salt—no, I'll take my punishment as it comes.
Some don't like that kind of talk, but they's the worst

of all: looking for pasture when it's time to plow,
soft in the chin while they cinch up their brows.
Well, I guess it's time to stop flappin'
and slap some supper on. Ain't no tellin'

what y'all 'll call food when the good Lord
calls me home. Or when ol' horny-head calls me
into his ring to fight for my everlasting soul.
He does that, he better watch his ass, let me tell you.

He thinks he's raised hell—huh, he ain't seen nuthin' yet.

Discomfort and Its Undoing

Discomfort, mere (*ha, mere*) discomfort, never mind pain, discomfort alone will make of us irritable idiots, men and women who take the easy road, the wrong road, the road that leads to trouble. And we will curse the road for being the way it is, and our feet for wearing such sad, disintegrating shoes.

And when we get to the end of that road, or a stopping-place of realization, we will know it was the wrong way, and everything will be met with disgust, revulsion, the inclination to swallow all beauty and spew. The dissatisfaction of living will make our tongues unable to stand the taste of our own mouths. We will spit in the dust and get the spit on ourselves and glare at the sun as though it were the bright idea behind all this.

Unless. Unless something gets in the way of our anger. Some messenger who intersects us: a tangerine for instance, just a tad overripe, forgotten at the bottom of the bag, might be the hook which untangles everything that went wrong. Then, as though peeling back a rind, the mind will section by section come clear. The senses will conduct the weather's music, and to their liking, even if the clouds hang heavy and low.

A foul wind might dog us, might drive us ever more contracted into ourselves, but we won't wish it ill. We'll lick our lips and lower our heads, listen to its whistle and commit it to memory. We'll remember our summer together, and say *thanks, I know the going is rough, but you breathe for something too; hold on a second while I open my chest—there, climb on in and I'll carry you home.*

Hunting for Good

All day he has walked
through the woods with his gun.

He has had the chance to kill.
Good chances, feathery, tufted.

He has raised his gun and lowered it,
leaving the bullets in their bed.

Now he takes his hands
to lesser killing in the garden.

Slaps his mind for thinking
leaflife somehow lesser.

At dinner his cat
jumps on the table.

Sniffs his plate, drops her tail,
droops and trots away.

As he retires to bed,
he looks out the window
and catches her
approaching a nest.

Bangs the glass,
scares her back,
yells her down,
but he knows.

She will crouch at the base of the tree.
She will wait for the reading lamp's dark.
She will slither up the bark in his sleep.

He'll wake to his body, then to his
knowledge, and question whether
a good man would put her down.

Deep Gap Creek

We were walking along the crick, on top of it, the water low, the stones dry and right for stepping, thinking of ticks and diseases and longing to be home, here or someplace like it, mountainous, but these mountains were too many, too big, too sky-bruising for a boy from Florida and a girl from Texas, Minnesota, Iowa, Iran.

Our hearts moseyed up to Virginia where the hills looked like something a life could climb. New York was for money and taking a beating and eating the old dishes whose recipes have disappeared from their lands. Toughing it, so the knees wouldn't complain when they finally sunk into dilapidated gardens. A farmer's a good thing but no replacement for a carrot you just pulled to share.

Cinnamon Addie padded from bank to bank, delighting in the Labradetter scent-scape our noses would never comprehend. We wanted to ask her: what do our hands tell you of our lives? How do you know when a place wants you to stop and roll in the grass? To pick that plot and belong? Is it any coincidence that when pain descends, you show up and it thaws? Why the musty corners of everything? Is old pee really so magnificent?

We crawled up the bank. Addie acquiesced for a treat. Were your feet bare? I want now, as I wanted then, to rub them, run my thumb along the instep, squeeze the diminutive heel. What is it about mountains that gives a boy of beaches and a girl of cornfields the sense of a common dream? But small ones. The kind that fit in the view from the kitchen window, one doing dishes, the other drying.

The kind that remind you of each in the other, two hearts where one was, and why stop there—the kind that remind you of the earth in your heart without blocking out the light.

Holding Fort

The wind has fingers—
they pry at your zippers,
your pockets, your pores.

Ability and Restraint

after Geoffrey Hill

I

Recognize the damned
among your friends
and your friends
among the damned,
and the blessing
of the recognition
when it comes to you,
whether you looked for it
or not. Though human
is where we live and die,
it is just the beginning
of the world. Ah,
to ache and suffer through it,
and sense within the ache
the ability to enjoy,
not the ache, but being
where ache happens.

II

The heart will
have its way with you.
The mind is no match.
Keep your head down.
Ignore that stone
in your chest, beating
like it wants to break.
Force your way through
ignorance to awareness.
Kill the mice, don't
feed them. So what
if each sprung trap
snuffs another
squeak inside you?
Though revelation may
arrive like a trainwreck,
though life may
break you into love,
let the pressure build.

A Place

for Safora Ray and Wendell Berry

If we've never known home,
how do we get there
aside from the way we get everywhere,
the way we receive looks that say *keep moving,*
the way we understand those looks
and keep going until one day,
we look around,
take stock and think *yes,*
this must be what it feels like to belong.

Only to be betrayed by that feeling
when our foreignness shows itself,
makes itself plain,
and that old itch to move on
sends us into the closets, packing.

There must be a place
where this cycle can be broken,
a place where the habit of homelessness
can be traded in for a habit of homemaking,
but I've not yet found it,
and the buses every day
are full of others who haven't either;

the boundaries of nations
are crossed one broken spirit at a time,
and the promises of prosperity
are buried in their rhetorical graves,
tossed in the ditches
for the scavengers to try their luck.

They must have a tougher stomach than me,
for I—I will not handle shit
shovelful after another
if it isn't leading toward something like manure,
and not just any pile, but a pile on a farm,
or in the hands of someone
who knows how to put it to beneficial use.

I will not sell my mind one office day at a time
until there is little left of it to otherwise contribute.

I will sell it only so long as it takes to tear it
from the pockets of rich, unkindly men,
men who will never take the time to know me
or the countless other downgraded souls
who fluff their expensive pillows
and their pillowy pretensions of greatness.

And then I will move on
from this place which is not home.

I will move toward the place
that I have been imagining with my heart,
and the heart of my wife,
and the hearts of the animals in our care,
and the hearts of the children
who will be born there,
the children who will be raised there
and will always know
what it means to say home,
even if that sense of home
should one day go off with them,
should haunt them through their travels,
should become for them, as it is for me:

a place where one may send down roots
by tending to the roots of one's sustenance;
a place where one takes the time
to get to know one's neighbors,
and not only the neighbors
who speak with the human tongue;

a place where everything we need
is within walking distance,
or if it isn't yet,
it's within our ability
and our plans to make it so;

a place where one slowly accumulates
the lay of the land and its creatures—
its patterns, its cycles,
its stages and seasons—
and turns that living landscape
into the shape of one's own thinking;

a place where economy
is what one does with what one has,
and the tools we use
are tools we know how to fix or do without;

a place where what goes into the air
is treated like what goes into one's breath;
a place where what goes into the ground
is treated like food for one's mother;
a place where the graves are dug by hand
for creatures we have known and loved;
a place where the rivers of water
are as important as the rivers of blood;

a place where waste
is what comes out of the body
and is otherwise to be avoided;
a place where limitations are indications
of a properly inhabited scale;
a place where mistakes
are signs of where there is work to do,
and one attends to each mistake
as to an open wound;

a place where one listens
to what the place asks
of those who would make it home,
and responds with the effort
of those who would keep it home
for generations to come;

a place where the rift of placelessness
can begin to close and heal,
and people, people like us,
can share with it, can be with it
in reverent acts of earnest care
what we can't say about it,
what we can't know about it,
what we can only,
finally,
feel
about the place
that is slowly, surely, sweetly, achingly
forming in my mind.

How It Happens

How many times in the age of a tree
the wind says to the wind
in the leaf and the leaf in the wind
come out—we have mouths
to feed—come out—we have ground
to cover—come out to make room
for the others—come out
and come along.

And every time that piano note
on the breath of a finger
enters the body of the one beside it
and it further
and the room fills
with the blooming forest of a chord
I think it's a perfectly good thing to die.

Chopping Wood

I liked going out in the rain,
so much rain in that land of green hills,
evergreens and infections of the lung,
liked stepping through puddles
in my once water-resistant boots
as I made my way to the woodshed
where I'd pull the rusty light-cord,
check for spiders, then eye the piles,
one of oak, several of fir, and pick
the next victims for our old-fashioned,
wood-burning stove. Then I'd carry the logs
to the chopping block and drop them,
not carelessly, but less concerned
with the way they'd lie than the way they fell,
and wonder about the woodsman who felled them,
how he'd ponder bringing them down from the sky
and selling them by the cord,
whether the land was his or he bought them,
walking through and showing which,
spray-painting the bark to remember.

Then I'd pick up the logs
and place them on the block,
this time with care so they wouldn't fall
and would offer me their broadest face
to swing my favorite axe down into.
And I'd begin the work
that took me out in the rain in joy:
I'd measure my paces back from the block
(a two-hundred fir by my quick reckoning),
I'd lower my hands along the shaft,
swing the axe over my head
and throw some muscle into the chop.

And if the log was placed right,
if the swing was hard enough,
if hand and eye, mind and muscle
came together in perfect concert,
the log would split, the blade would embed
ever so slightly in the face of the block,
and I'd place my sole on the edge of that old fir,
and use the leverage of my body
to bring the axe-glint back into the light.

And if any one of those things was off,
the axe would stick in the little log
and I'd lift it, axe and all, over my head,
and come crashing down
and crashing down,
the sound like a gunshot, until it split.
Or the blade would stick in the block,
and I'd have to tease it side to side
while I tried to coax it out.
An hour's rain later, out it would come,
the wood would be split,
and I'd pile it in my arms, careful of splinters,
then carry it in to warm the bodies,
the lives of my wife and children.

Once, I missed the log and the block entirely,
and the blade glanced off my shin,
but made no damage,
no cut, not even a bruise,
and I thought of how easily
the bone would have splintered.
I felt pain at the thought of being a tree
subject to the woodsman's expertise,
the loss of shade that was respite
to so many creatures,
the nests woven
high up in the swaying branches,

the resting spots for migrants,
playgrounds for squirrels, haunts for owls
whose screeches scorched us in our beds,
the cats alert with God only knows in their ears.

And I thought of the grave
I dug on that property,
larger than a man's grave,
the size of a woman and child, I thought,
as I dug through black dirt into grey clay
that didn't want to be dug,
my muscles tiring,
the sky grumbling,
the earth refusing the shovel,
the mother llama looking on
and moaning low
as her child's body
decomposed under the tarp.

Sleeping

after George Oppen

under the blanket
we seem to be

the dream
of something

it isn't earthly
she doesn't

moan like that
in life

Death, a Wife, and a Life of Broken Rules

I

Is it because I'm tired tonight
that I don't want to think of death,

my lifelong confidante,
the ear in me that has no flesh,

that never had a drop of blood
to spill between some crack in the desert—

the ear that, as far as the eye can tell,
is not here, but is nonetheless wholly listening?

II

Whatever the reason, I must decline.
No, my friend, I do not want

a glass of wine with you,
a tray of cheeses, fine cuts of meat;

I do not want to shove you in my mouth
and savor your descent into my bowels.

III

I want the simplicity of water tinged
with the minerals of my hometown,

the familiar blend of sulfur, iron and arsenic
that makes hotel water taste wrong.

IV

I want a joke and the knowing laughter
that swells in wit born of sorrow,

sorrow that bites and leaves a mark
that mars every flawless mirror.

V

I want a broken back that has just experienced
an uncommon day of relief,

a spine stretching towards the heavens
that doesn't recoil in pain.

VI

I want to know why the pigment in that painting
made me feel the way I do. I want to live
another night in the company of my wife's skin.

I want the moment when her shades of cream
conspired to teach me what I could never have
taught myself about the complexities of snow.

VII

I close my eyes and I am there;
she is next to me and we are happy;

the future is a condition
apart from our time together.

VIII

They tell me I am foolish to dwell, that there is
no life in death and no bringing back what's gone.
But I tell you they don't know everything,

and life is a breaker of rules—what my heart
does with me when I turn myself over to its aims
makes me a firm believer that love can do anything it wants.

IX

When I want to be with her,
all I have to do is sit like this
and close my eyes.

Then it's easy, it's like
I've awoken in the night
and all I have to do

is peel back the covers
and feel my way to her
through the dark.

Midlife: Too Early for an *Ars Poetica*

after Czeslaw Milosz

The purpose is, oh purpose was,
if poetry had one and it went down like a tonic
for the ache of living in these bodies
that fall from women into the earth,
goodbye slick wombs of grace,
how effortless to say something,
how difficult to live it

the houses we are in poems in art
in the shedding of selves in being oneself
open open open

come in, don't mind
the draft and dung,
the deed says *all who happen through*
and the doors have no locks
and the hinges have no doors
and soon the walls are breaking apart
into trees, oh ancient forest.

Late Night Possibilities

I

You could close your eyes,
your neck dripping with sweat
in the late September heat.

II

You could dream
of driving somewhere,
quickly,

of horns and flashing lights
trying to guide you
toward your destination.

III

You could waver between
the dream state and waking state
where sparks shower your face

from the side of the car
shearing the guard rail,
the guard rail shearing the car.

IV

Your foot could become
heavy with sleep

and your hands could fall
away from the wheel

and your body could plow
into the night

with no concern
for laws or lanes

or the deer trying to herd her young
safely to the other side.

V

You could be seduced
by 75-mph winds
whistling something dangerous in your ear

and you could reach for the wheel
like the belly of a lover
who's leaving you too soon

and you could pull her back to you
only to spin around
and flip over twice—earth, sky, earth, sky.

VI

You could wake your friend
in the passenger seat
to tell him what happened.

VII

You could pull your other friend
from the screaming hole
in the back window

with blood
and glass in flesh
and no one to blame but yourself

for listening to your mind
when it said *it's time*
you're tired

let's go.

Limited Uses

Until the sparrow
struggling upon the ground
catches your eye
and adopts you as something useful.

Until you feed it hourly
dawn to dusk
and hold it against your breast
like a part of your heart
struggling to get back in.

Until you learn
to tamp down your motherly instinct
lest the little sliver
spend its life
tethered to your ribcage.

Until it's more complicated than that:
my wife's hand was a refuge;
the sparrow was dying;
death uncloaked itself
in the sparse feather development—

in the end, little Chickpea
lost her appetite: a small fluttering
of the wings, all that was left
of her never-to-be-taken flight.

Safora held her and kissed her
as she cried, crouched against the tile wall,
and I watered the day with grief, too.

Little Chickpea opened her eyes
for the first time that morning
and flew from her body,
a gift that widened the circle of us
for weeks—thirteen grams
of exquisite creation
we carried and buried and marked with her perch,

on either end a glittering stone.

Preparation

My dog bit a bee,
spit it out,
no sign of stung.

A lesson for the poet
who bites at life
eager to be bit back.

Contrary to no one's belief
the bee's wings were not spun
of marigolds and mead.

But something is,
I've heard the rising
bread it breathes,

the dying wheat
that smells
of hunger—

my dog, I watch her
nose apart
the blades of grass

and catch the scents
that fall like petals
from the heels of wind,

a woman she tracks
like an old,
restless friend.

The Blooming Noses

Flowers, these people are flowers who can brace the wind of a winter's day, but not the wind of a bullet. Most aim is bad despite the years of training and most rubber bullets will miss, but the few that don't will scatter the majority into hiding, the rebels into hills, while dissidents shiver in abandoned buildings, heating beans over small blue flames. Some of the shooters will want to change sides, but will be bound to abide by the pullers of strings.

Strings of the purse, not strings of the heart. Strings that say plant the drugs in the pocket and watch the felony grow. Mace the face and watch the dissent shrivel into tears. Rough up for good measure, but not in front of the camera, and not the pretty female face or the old face or the rest of the faces where it's blatantly visible. A kidney shot for the mouthy ones and a stomach jab to widen the eyes of the highly educated.

Raid the encampment in the middle of the night and make a racket that would make your scalp-seeking ancestors proud. Burn the library and break the cookware. Accost the medics, dump their stores into the sewers. Herd them all like sleepy cattle. Hint at slaughter. Make them feel that their life is in danger and tell them that you're doing it for their own good. Their hygiene has been declared a public hazard and their health is in jeopardy in more ways than one.

This is the land of baby powder, not the land of shit and mud. This is the land of tightly-controlled chemical stimulation and the doctors are standing by to diagnose your condition. The pharmacists are standing by to fill your order. It's time to put away the protests and pick up your belongings and head up the mountain of debt. It's time to think of your children in the present and forget about a nebulous future.

It's time to face the facts of your position and make your journey along the predefined routes. And if you insist on questioning rules, if you insist on picking at scabs, then it will be time to call in the hounds, and there is nowhere left on earth that escapes our gaze for long. If we have to hunt you down, we will, and then it will be time to teach you a lesson.

Then it will be time to taste the blood of a traitor. Then it will be time for locked doors, brutal beatings, and the torturous hands of power. Then it will be time to wake up day after day and smell the bloody, blooming noses. And *then* time will switch sides. *Then* it will be time to listen to the blood in our bodies, the blood down our faces, the blood on our hands, and feel our hearts pump with the truth of what the blood tells us to do.

In America We Long For

A savior because countries die,
because death drags
her shadow
through the soil

and no one knows her name
or what she wants
when she sings the bottom
of the heart to sleep

and blows two quick
darts of breath
that snuff out
the candles of our eyes.

In the Dawn

for John Berryman

Nobody in the dawn. It hasn't yet assembled
        the people in its psalm.
If a voice has no body, does it need an ear?
        Does the blood carry
its own crosses as it flickers in the flesh
        in search of nothing,
the woman it is, a walking yard of graves?
        She is not for loving,
as if love were the sharp tip of purpose
        piercing, cutting away
the civilizations bacteria build on bone.
        But loving does fit in,
if fitting means being strung along an act
        of service: the guitar
talks back to the fingers, the world whispers
        to the living: touch
until the noise and feel coalesce, reveal
        the music made when
strings and fingers lock as lovers
        knocking the headboard
against the wall, a thousand times
        its rhythmic pulse
that gives the hour what it wanted when
        it made the bodies
and made them ache and put them together
        for love or what
might ever come of living in the dawn.

Last Call

God coughed, and the gatekeeper groaned.
The usual trickle of ascendants
through God's ribs, the bars of heaven,
had been drying up for centuries,
and who could blame them?
The animals kept becoming
animals and elements,
women turned into horses,
men into half-decent ideas,
and everyone was stripped
of sorrow and suffering
as blood gave earth back its salt.

You'd get a handful of bible thumpers
whose fear forbade the good life
in favor of sickly virtue,
holes in their shoes
and the promises of hell
hot as coals on their tongues,
but you could count on them
for a half-dead joke
and a really good glass of water.

You'd get a woman who raised ten children
she didn't have the sex to bear
but who, in the unplanned hours
on any given, could milk
the neighbor's goats for chèvre,
nurse a newbie, solve for x,
brush five heads, inspect ten
gaping mouths blackspotted
by heredity and McDonalds.

There were others—in his journal
the gatekeeper recorded
the storied ages and ordered species
that have all but been wiped from our cells,
but most, even those who qualified
to spend eternity repeating
the moment when the wine kicks in,
teaching Bach new ways to jam,
chose not to attend.

They found heaven where they were,
made it in their own
deluded image,
and they liked it dirty,
themselves the product of dirt,
an earth moonlighting as human,
and this, of all things
worth a half-wit's
attempt at contemplation,
they were just beginning to consider.

The heavenmakers, as he called them,
liked their mirrors tarnished,
the glass opaque,
the silver flaking at the corners,
antiques kept because
they know how to reflect
without buying into appearances.

And with their newfound powers
the heavenmakers smoothed their wrinkles,
shrunk their ankles, made breasts
and bums identical twins,
but left the scars, the stories of war,

and over the light behind the bar—
the beer dark for the meek
and light for the cheap—
they often hung an inappropriate remark.

Of course some idiot would come along,
have too many and stir up
some nonsense about offense to God,
but God was not angry because
God did not playact as human behavior,
and only simpletons
thought God was anything other
than the precision of is;

as if being everything wasn't enough;
as if, despite universes happening
in a nanostretch of God's graces,
God still had reason to be
sat at a stool and pissed off,
a pen low-on-ink
in her three-fingered hand,
crossing off names from heaven.

Terms of Belonging

We would do well to remember
that what we detect is not nature on inhuman terms,
or inhuman terms alone,
not nature herself, some might say—not I—
but nature as grasped by our capacities of understanding,
nature as grasped by nature in human form.

God retreats inasmuch as attention retreats from God,
but swing the lantern of attention back,
there, under the leaves, in the leaves themselves,
in various states of decay, soil is being born,
the mother of soil is delivering
her only child.

Sometimes the Work Comes to You

A herd of horses gathered outside my cabin, their hoofbeats steady as a bonfire crackling green logs. At the same time I could hear them bent to the earth, nipping the young grass. It was the wrong season. I wore two sweaters. In my dream, from across the lake, a wolf howled to remind me of a wound left open in the soul. My blood flew with his howl. Then it turned in the air like a flock of pigeons and came back. The wolf sat beside me and watched. I asked to borrow his nose.

Caught the scent of decay and followed it to my heart.
A ruin of promises I never kept.
Lifted a lie and a pup with my eyes looked back.
I knew which poem he was, and lowered my hand to feed him.

He said it was time to stop writing poems and start living them.
A crow cawed in agreement.
A squirrel dug up a nut and brought it for courage.
I ate it and my eyes became light.

When I woke I could still hear the horses grazing. I went out to look and an angry wind blew leaves that bit the ground. The mountain dropped rocks, click-clack, into the valley. No birds at the feeders, ice on the day's tongue. I put on another sweater, thick gloves. My last piece of oak in the woodstove. It was time for work. I sat in the lap of the earth and closed my eyes. The wolf howled and I could feel it in my throat.

Regeneration

Rising from the wheelchair,
my legs hold me up—
two withered twigs.

I love dead wood,
the way it keeps daring
lightning to strike again.

And I love lightning,
the way it keeps reminding
the heart it's on fire.

Acknowledgements

Wholehearted thanks to the editors and judges of the following publications for giving the poems below their first moments in the light.

Periodicals

Lodestone Journal: "What These Senses Can Do," "Note with the Hand I Sent You," "On Compassion," "The Bloody Medium," "Bounty," "How It Happens"

Eyewear Publishing: "The Seven Hundred Sights in a Horse"

Rat's Ass Review: "When to Reveal"

Terrene: "Something We Were Supposed to Do," "Deep Gap Creek," "Terms of Belonging"

Sixfold: "Listening," "They Used to Be Things," "The Music of As Is," "Proximity," "The Bird," "Discomfort and its Undoing," "Chopping Wood," "Death, a Wife, and a Life of Broken Rules," "Late Night Possibilities," "The Blooming Noses"

Low Rent: "Old Amber Eyes"

Fantastic Floridas: "Arc of an Afternoon," "Dreaming of Panthers"

Ink, Sweat & Tears: "A Neighborhood of Vertebrae"

Amaryllis: "Tolerance"

The Matador Review: "Way of the Bear"

Yellow Chair Review: "Despair"

The American Scholar: "Forbidden Diamonds," "Thanksgiving with Vegetarians," "Just a Moment," "I Saw Myself in the Black Car"

Fourth & Sycamore: "Two Postcards to Myself from April 1, 2017," "Because Meaning Physics Life"

One: "When You Lost It"

MadHat Lit: "Kifka"

The Paragon Journal: "The Word Want"

The Coil: "Guard Dog," "One Day Becomes Forever"

Noble/Gas Qtrly: "The Lightbulb," "The Enmity Between Spiders and Bees"

Star 82: "Through the Veil"

Quail Bell Magazine: "A Thousand Palms a Day"

Horseshoes & Hand Grenades: "Animalis," "Last Call"

Esque Mag: "The Need for a Sickly Body to Rebel: All It Takes is One Overambitious Limb"

1932: "Blue Hurricane"

Lit.Cat: "Thank You"

Fugue: "Four Contracting Sentences and Two Scenes that Won't Comply"

Weatherbeaten Lit: "Spring Again," "Holding Fort," "Midlife: Too Early for an *Ars Poetica*"

Young Ravens: "Gravestones"

Sheila-Na-Gig: "Someone's Ashes," "Ability and Restraint"

Scintilla: "Hunting for Good"

Concis: "In the Dawn"

Anthologies

Next Line, Please: "Just a Moment," Cornell University Press (2018), Edited by · David Lehman, with Angela Ball

Persona Non Grata: "Listening," Fly on the Wall Poetry Press (2018), Edited by Isabelle Kenyon

[insert yourself here]: "Arc of an Afternoon," The Paragon (2017), Edited by Austin Shay

Awards

"Four Contracting Sentences and Two Scenes that Won't Comply," The Ron McFarland Poetry Prize, **Fugue**, chosen by Pulitzer laureate Claudia Emerson

"The Seven Hundred Sights in a Horse," The Fortnight Poetry Prize, **Eyewear Publishing**, chosen by senior editor Rosanna Hildyard

"A Place," Whisper River Poetry Prize, chosen by an anonymous benefactor

My sincere and abiding thanks to everyone who helped the work find its way up; your friendship, care and inspiration will be held in an enduring gratitude: Rilke and Rumi, who opened the floodgates and baptized me in poetry's waters; Wendell Berry, who instilled in me an understanding that writing should always carry affection's flame, even in protest, outrage and despair; my first readers, Ashley Wood and Stanley Nightingale, who made the years of struggle feel worthwhile; my first loves, Michelle, Raina and Nadine— though the rooms you left in my heart grow dusty, I walk through them in wonder as one would walk through a field of stars; my family, for the fire in my blood and everything it took to feed it; Pete Marsh, for teaching me the value and hard work of building character; my teachers, Loren-Paul Caplin, Sandeep Chatterjeek, Mazie Lane, Bob O'Hearn, Lisa Jarnot, David Lehman, Leonard Schwartz, Jenny Boully, and Kevin Higgins, who showed me the way and guided a novice when he needed assistance; my friends, Nick, Chris, Mike and Christian, who supported a fool on a fool's mission; Columbia University, for the libraries and education; Poets House, Alabaster Books, East Village Books and the Strand, my oases in the apple; *Heartland*, for giving me hope amidst the physical crises; my listserv and poetry groups, where I cut my teeth and learned the art, more often than not, through osmosis: *Yearning, Adyashanti Satsang, Poetry for Thought, Images-Inscript, Buddhist Wellness, Irony Waves, Poetic License, Worldwide Wordsmiths, Poetics, Whisper River, Modern Poetry, Next Line Please, Rat's Ass Review, Wryting, Now Poetry, British & Irish Poets, Over the Edge* and *Poets Abroad*; the editors of the journals and anthologies who first gave me a chance, notably Saul Williams, Claudia Emerson, and the teams at *Sixfold* and *Lodestone*; my manuscript advisors, Rosanna Hildyard, Evy Zen, Natalie Eilbert, Jo Burns, Audrey Molloy, Joshua Decker, Paul Michelsen, Stephen Power, Stephanie Roberts, Emily Brandt, Vincent DiGirolamo and Esther Smith, for keeping me honest and nimble, apologies for the torture; Shaunna Russell, for the amazing cover; William Stafford and the folks at Graywolf, for the epigraph; the rockstars at Diode Editions, Patty Paine, Law Alsobrook, and Zoe Shankle Donald, for keeping my dream alive; the unsayable, for being song; everyone I forgot, forgive this humble human; Rascal and Addie, my canine brother and sister, woof woof, paw, lick, bottomless bags of treats and every day beside you; and Safora, my darling wife—you, most of all, gave these poems true heart.

Ricky Ray was born in Florida and educated at Columbia University. He is the founding editor of *Rascal: a Journal of Ecology, Literature and Art*. His awards include the Cormac McCarthy Prize, the Ron McFarland Poetry Prize, the Fortnight Poetry Prize and a Whisper River Poetry Prize. His work has appeared widely in periodicals and anthologies, including *The American Scholar, The Matador Review, Amaryllis, Scintilla* and *Fugue*. He lives in Harlem with his wife, three cats, and a Labradetter. Their bed is frequently overcrowded.